Perversery Rhymes

21st Century American Mother Goose

Volume 1

By Hoby Gilman

In the hallowed tradition of Mother Goose, Perversery Rhymes memorializes today's history lessons for hundreds of generations to come.

perverse

adjective

per·verse | \ (ˌ)pər-ˈvərs , ˈpər-ˌvərs \

obstinate in opposing what is right, reasonable, or accepted : WRONGHEADED

This collection of rhymes is dedicated
to life, liberty, and the pursuit of happiness.

Table of Contents

Archway Publishing books may be ordered through booksellers or by contacting:

Archway Publishing
1663 Liberty Drive
Bloomington, IN 47403
www.archwaypublishing.com
844.669.3957

ISBN: 978-1-4808-9657-4 (hc)
ISBN: 978-1-4808-9673-4 (e)

Printed in the United States of America.

Archway Publishing rev. date: 10/28/2020

ARCHWAY
PUBLISHING

Oh where, oh where has our government fled?
Oh where, oh where can it be?
Separation of powers and oversight dead;
Oh where, oh where can it be?

Cadet Bone Spurs

Donny Bone Spur pumpkin pie
Kissed the girls and made them lie
But when the boys got on the boat
Donny showed his doctor’s note

Dumb Dumb Cheeto Sheep

Dumb Dumb Don Trump, have
you any fools?
Yes, sir, yes, sir, three states full
One full of badgers
And one with Great Lakes
And one full of orange crops
Those were three mistakes

Five Little Piggies

This little piggy got Interior
This little piggy got Commerce
This little piggy took EPA
This little piggy took HHS
And this little piggy went
"Wee wee wee" all the way to the bank

This Ryan Zinke flew the big parks
This Wilbur Ross got sued
This Tommy Price took nice planes
This Scott Pruitt did too
And this Steve Mnuchin went
"Cha-ching cha-ching cha-ching" on his honeymoon

·Covfefe!·

Covfefe

Sent a tweet, sent a tweet, no forethought
Should have double-checked, but you forgot
Typed it, liked it, and sent it with glee
The word *covfefe* spread virally

Little Stephen Miller

Little Stephen Miller sat in his cellar
Drawing up his scheme
Lock up their mamas
Lock up their papas
And laugh as the little kids scream!

Bittery Twittery

Bittery Twittery Twit
The brat flew into a snit
He tweeted a ton
And still he's not done
Bittery Twittery Twit

Be Best

First Lady, First Lady, your motto is sullied
Your husband has slandered the people he's bullied
Were you serious, or was it in jest
When you proclaimed all should *be best*?

MAGA
MAGA
MAGA
MAGA
MAGA
MAGA
MAGA
MAGA
MAGA

Dumpy Trumpy

Dumpy Trumpy wanted his wall
Dumpy Trumpy wanted it tall
Thirty-five days tweeting from his commode
Left public servants unpaid and furloughed

Moscow Mitch

Complicity, duplicity, Moscow Mitch
Ignores bills that guard our votes
Sometimes smiles, sometimes gloats
Complicity, duplicity, Moscow Mitch

Extortion

Nancy, Nancy, Clapping Fancy

Nancy, Nancy, clapping fancy
How do your charges grow?
No protocol on that phone call
And all wrapped up with a bow

Old Giuliani

Old Giuliani, he played one
He bamboozled on my thumb
With a Ukraine-bungled scheme
Give the Fox a bone
He butt dialed a newsman's phone

Old Kellyanne, she played two
She bamboozled on my shoe
With a this, that, alternative fact,
Give the Fox a bone
She tried to sell Ivanka's clothes

Old Don Junior, he played three
He bamboozled on my knee
With a bad joke, hates the "woke"
Give the Fox a bone
He's the king of all self-owns

Old Ivanka, she played four
She bamboozled at my door
With her emails and book fails
Give the Fox a bone
She started a biz on Daddy's loan

Old Jared Kush, he played five
He bamboozled on my hive
With a clearance to secrets
Give the Fox a bone
He was exposed in Mueller's probe

Old Eric Trump, he played six
He bamboozled on my sticks
With cancer kids on the skids
Give the Fox a bone
He wants to be his daddy's clone

Old Steve Bannon, he played seven
He bamboozled up to heaven
With his data breach and hate speech
Give the Fox a bone
He squealed on old Roger Stone

Old Ben Carson, he played eight
He bamboozled on my gate
With fake glory and stories
Give the Fox a bone
He denied the Dreamers' loans

Old Manafort, he played nine
He bamboozled on my spine
With the dossier, kickback pay
Give the Fox a bone
He is jailed but won't atone

Old Giuliani, he played ten
He bamboozled once again
With drug ties and virus lies
Give the Fox a bone
He had his reputation blown

Yankee Donald

Yankee Donald came to town
Riding his inheritance
Wore his red tie past his crotch
And called it utmost elegance

FOX

Huck and Spice

Huck and Spice, they shucked and jived
In myths and lies they wallowed
Spice wore down and left the town
In two years, Huck had followed

Spice took a chance and went to dance
With the stars on Monday night
Huck took some knocks for joining Fox
Where she hoaxed and lied outright

Whistle, Whistle

Whistle, whistle, secret star
How I wonder who you are
Warning us of just one crime
Many more but out of time
Thank you, thank you, secret star
How I wonder who you are

QUID PRO
QUO

Quid Pro Quo

Quid pro quo, quid pro quo
But who to believe? But who to believe?
Trump tried to keep the meeting discreet
But Rudy spoiled the ruse with a tweet
Did dumber criminals you ever meet
Than quid pro quo?

Pop! Goes the Beer Can

Christine braved the testimony
But Lindsey's not her fan
That's the way politics go
Pop! Goes the beer can

Deb and Julie named his crime
GOP stuck to their plan
That's the way politics go
Pop! Goes the beer can

True
Heroic
Tales

Tough John Bolton

Tough John Bolton
Come and get sworn
Rudy's in Ukraine
And Schiff is forlorn
But where is the man
Who secured our defense?
Writing a book at our expense

Old Mother Gantry

Old Mother Gantry went to Dollar Pantry
To get her poor kids some bread
But to her chagrin
SNAP bennies rescind
So her kids went hungry to bed

USA

One, Two

One, two
DiBlasio's through
Three, four
Kirsten's out the door
Five, six
Castro's nixed
Seven, eight
Beto's fate
Nine, ten
So long, Williamson
Eleven, twelve
Kamala's hell
Thirteen, fourteen
There goes Cory
Fifteen, sixteen
Who was Inslee?
Seventeen, eighteen
Yang's not seen
Nineteen, twenty
Still aplenty
Twenty-one and twenty-two
Pete and Mike, "Adieu!"
Twenty-three and twenty-four
Amy couldn't score
Twenty-five and twenty-six
Warren's out of tricks
Twenty-seven and twenty-
eight
Tulsi's in this late
Twenty-nine and thirty
Biden or Bernie?

Ring Around the Rona

Pandemics are such nonsense
Close down biodefense
Ashes! Ashes!
We'll all be fine!

Only fifteen here are sick
We'll make it zero quick
Ashes! Ashes!
We'll all be fine!

Dems pass Families First Bill
Junior says they're the worst still
Ashes! Ashes!
We'll all be fine!

After Trump's late insistence
We keep our social distance
Ashes! Ashes!
We all fall down!

Liesol

The Itsy-Bitsy Virus

The itsy-bitsy virus
Trump was asked about:
Down a lil Lysol
And wash the virus out
Out comes the sun
And takes away the pain
And the itsy-bitsy virus
Will never kill again

Bunker Boy

Bunker Boy, Bunker Boy,
Where have you been?
In my dark bunker
Away from smoke screen

Bunker Boy, Bunker Boy,
What did you there?
Ordered up tear gas
On citizens who care

Bunker Boy, Bunker Boy,
Where have you been?
Escorted to church
Haven't you seen?

Bunker Boy, Bunker Boy,
What did you there?
Held up some book
But said no prayer

For want of two votes, witnesses were lost
For want of witnesses, the trial was lost
For want of the trial, the truth was lost
For want of the truth, justice was lost
For want of justice, democracy was lost
And all for the want of two lousy votes

When did we quit putting sanctimonious, hypocritical figures in their place? The British used to inscribe these controversies into the nursery rhymes of Mother Goose so that these crimes and transgressions would be remembered throughout history. *Perversery Rhymes* enshrines current American fakers, hoaxers, and shams in their own children's book, ensuring that they, too, will live on in infamy. Read about Tough John Bolton, Little Stephen Miller, Moscow Mitch, Cadet Bone Spurs, and their accomplices.

Parental discretion strongly advised.

Visit us at PerverseryRhymes.com.